cooking the THAI way

A spicy sweet and sour dipping sauce goes well with marinated chicken, while *satay* is delicious with either peanut or cucumber sauce. (Recipes on pages 38 and 39.)

cooking the
THAI way

SUPENN HARRISON & JUDY MONROE

PHOTOGRAPHS BY ROBERT L. & DIANE WOLFE

easy menu
ethnic
cookbooks

Lerner Publications Company ▪ Minneapolis

Editor: Vicki Revsbech
Drawings and Map by Jeanette Swofford

Photographs on pages 8 and 10 courtesy of the
Tourism Authority of Thailand.

The page border for this book is an Asian elephant, an animal
native to Thailand. For centuries the Thai have considered the
white elephant to be sacred.

To all my customers, who love Thai food – S.H.

To my family, with love – J.M.

Library of Congress Cataloging-in-Publication Data

Harrison, Supenn.
　　Cooking the Thai way.

　　(Easy menu ethnic cookbooks)
　　Includes index.
　　Summary: An introduction to the cooking of Thailand
including such recipes as lemon chicken soup, satay, and
Thai egg rolls. Also includes information on the
history, geography, customs, and people of Thailand.
　　1. Cookery, Thai—Juvenile literature. 2. Thailand—
Social life and customs—Juvenile literature. [1. Cook-
ery, Thai. 2. Thailand—Social life and customs]
I. Monroe, Judy. II. Wolfe, Robert L., ill. III. Wolfe,
Diane, ill. IV. Title. V. Series.
TX724.5.T5H37　1986　　　641.59593　　　85-23208
ISBN 0-8225-0917-2 (lib. bdg.)

Manufactured in the United States of America

1　2　3　4　5　6　7　8　9　10　95　94　93　92　91　90　89　88　87　86

In Thailand, fresh lemon is used in both shrimp and mushroom soup *(front)* and lemon chicken soup *(back)*. (Recipes on pages 26 and 27.)

CONTENTS

Tanen Mountains

Chiang Mai

Fruit

Tobacco

Phetchabun Mountains

Mekong River

Corn

Bilauktaung Mountains

Chao Phraya River

Rice

Bangkok

Dong Rak Mountains

Cattle

Crab

Sugar Cane

Shrimp

Fish

Pineapples

Gulf of Thailand

Songkhla

Bananas

Hat Yai

Coconuts

■ **Northern Mountains**
□ **Khorat Plateau**
■ **Central Plain**
■ **Southern Peninsula**

Flag of Thailand

INTRODUCTION

For hundreds of years, the country of Thailand was known as Siam. Then in 1939, the name was changed to Thailand, or "Land of the Free." The Thai have never been ruled by a Western nation and are very proud of their independence. However, they are also open to ideas from other countries and are masters at blending the old with the new to create something altogether different that is unmistakeably Thai.

This talent for adaptation is most apparent in the arts, which have shown a great deal of Indian and, most recently, Western influence. The Thai are known the world over for their elaborate flower arrangements, fine handicrafts, and beautifully woven silks. They also consider food to be an art form and have borrowed ideas from other countries to create their own distinctive and delicious cuisine.

THE LAND

Thailand is located in Southeast Asia. It is surrounded by land on all but part of the southern side, where it borders on the Gulf of Thailand. Burma lies to the northwest, while Laos and Kampuchea (formerly Cambodia) make up the eastern border. Thailand's neighbor to the south is Malaysia, which forms the tip of the Malay Peninsula.

Thailand is made up of four very different regions. The Northern Mountain region in the northwest is a rugged land of thick forests and steep mountains, crisscrossed with many rivers. The Central Plain, a flat, broad expanse dominated by the mighty Chao Phraya River, is the country's most heavily populated region. This fertile plain is nicknamed "the Rice Bowl of Asia" for its large exports of high-quality rice. East of the Central Plain is the Khorat Plateau, a large, dry region with sandy soil. The Southern Peninsula, which borders on the western side of the Gulf of Thailand, is mostly tropical rain forest.

The vast majority of the Thai people are farmers who live in rural areas. Thailand has few large cities. The capital city of Bangkok, located in the Central Plain near the Gulf of Thailand, is the country's largest and most modern city, with a population of over five

Vendors sell fruits and vegetables from boats at this floating market on a *klong*, or canal, in Bangkok.

million. Bangkok was once called the "Venice of the East" because of its canals, or *klongs*, but the city has grown so rapidly that many of the *klongs* have been filled in to make room for buildings and highways. Other large cities in Thailand are Hat Yai and Songkhla in the south and Nakon Ratchasima in the northeast. Chiang Mai, the unofficial northern capital of Thailand, is internationally known for its exquisite handicrafts.

HISTORY

The original Thai people migrated from the Chinese province of Yunan in the 13th century. By the mid-14th century, the Thai, or Siamese as they were then known, controlled most of what would become Thailand. They established a central government and made Ayutthaya the capital.

The Siamese fought border wars almost continuously from the 14th century to the 17th century. In 1767, Burma captured and completely destroyed Ayutthaya, but the Siamese were not defeated. By 1777, the Burmese had been driven out and a new

capital had been established at Thonburi. In 1782, General Chakri became King Rama I and moved the capital to Bangkok.

During the second half of the 19th century, the Siamese were ruled by two very popular and influential kings, Rama IV and Rama V. These men, who were father and son, are remembered for their social reforms. In 1932, a bloodless revolution ended the king's absolute power, and a constitutional monarchy was established with both a king and a prime minister. The name of the country was changed to Thailand in 1939.

Since 1932, there have been many attempts to overthrow the government, and some of them have been successful. The country is located in an area of political unrest where conflicts still remain from the Vietnam War. In spite of this strife, however, Thailand is one of the most prosperous and stable countries in Southeast Asia, and the Thai people are united in their love and respect for their king, Rama IX, and proud to be "the Free People."

Some of the many fruits that grow in Thailand are on display at this stand in an open market.

THE FOOD

The Thai take their cuisine very seriously, and Thai cooks insist on using only the freshest and best quality ingredients. Their food is spicy and rich with a characteristic sweet/sour/salty taste, and it is usually beautifully arranged.

Over the years, Thai cuisine has been greatly influenced by other countries. But, whatever a recipe's origin, the Thai seem to be able to make it uniquely and deliciously their own. Chinese and Indian influences are especially strong in Thai cuisine. Stir-frying is a popular cooking technique that was adopted from China. Many Thai dishes have Chinese counterparts, which is not surprising because the original Thai came from southern China. The Chinese influence was made stronger by the trade that began between the two countries in the 19th century and by the many Chinese immigrants that settled in Thailand (then Siam).

The Indian influence on Thai cooking is most apparent in the curries, which are found in both cuisines. Although Thai curries are based on Indian curries, they are not the same because the Thai have substituted their own herbs and spices. Another similarity is the use of coconut milk with curries and with other dishes to mellow the flavors of the spices.

Thailand's terrain has isolated, to some degree, the four main regions of the country, and the cuisine of each region has its own unique characteristics. Grilled foods with wonderful, rich sauces are very popular in northeastern Thailand. Like their Laotian neighbors, Thais from this region prefer short-grained sticky rice to the long-grained rice that is common throughout the rest of Thailand. The central Thai are famous for their spicy cuisine, while those from the north prefer milder dishes. Fresh fish and shellfish from the Gulf of Thailand are favorites of the southern Thai. The south also has a huge range of curries, and chilis are eaten at every meal.

It is, however, the herbs, spices, and sauces that are the key ingredients in the cooking of every region in Thailand. The Thai flavor their food with black pepper, lemon juice, curry powder or paste, basil leaves, coriander, ginger root, and garlic. Sauces include oyster sauce, soy sauce, and fish sauce, the main ingredient in *nam pla prig*, which is a popular sauce that is sprinkled on nearly every dish.

HOLIDAY FEASTS IN THAILAND

I grew up in Thailand and have wonderful memories of the many festive holidays celebrated in my native country. The king's birthday is a national holiday, and on that day, each town is decorated with colored lights. At night we would walk around and try to find the most spectacular decorations. I remember the dinner table filled with traditional dishes and our family favorites. We always had steamed whole chicken with a hot pepper dipping sauce and sliced roast pig's head, also served with dipping sauce.

Like in most other countries, the Thai celebrate New Year's Day on the first of January, but we have traditions that are unique to Thailand. Every year my mother would make brown eggs. These hard boiled eggs cooked in soy sauce, sugar, fish sauce, and five spices symbolize a good life in the coming year. We would also eat delicious Thai egg rolls with *nam pla prig*. The table would be decorated with exquisite arrangements of many kinds of tropical fruit including bananas, coconuts, pineapples, and papayas.

Songkran is a three-day water festival in April. People douse each other with water and wash everything thoroughly in thanks for the rains and for good luck in the coming year. April is the hottest month in Thailand, so this is very refreshing and lots of fun! During Songkran, my mother would prepare a huge feast. The meal always included curries—usually yellow, our holiday color—and long noodles that symbolized long life.

Another favorite holiday in Thailand is Loy Krathong, which is celebrated in November. Each year we would make small bamboo boats and put lighted candles inside them. As we floated them down the river, we believed that the little boats carried away bad deeds and also paid honor to water spirits. Afterwards, we feasted on a large meal that included grilled chicken, fish, coconut, and egg yolks. Whatever the occasion, the Thai celebrate with family and good food!

BEFORE YOU BEGIN

Cooking any dish, plain or fancy, is easier and more fun if you are familiar with its ingredients. Thai cooking makes use of some ingredients that you may not know. You should also be familiar with the special terms that will be used in various recipes in this book. Therefore, *before* you start cooking any of the dishes in this book, study the following "dictionary" of special ingredients and terms very carefully. Then read through each recipe you want to try from beginning to end.

Now you are ready to shop for ingredients and to organize the cookware you will need. Once you have assembled everything, you can begin to cook. It is also very important to read *The Careful Cook* on page 44 before you start. Following these rules will make your cooking experience safe, fun, and easy.

COOKING UTENSILS

colander—A bowl-shaped dish with holes in it that is used for washing or draining food

pastry brush—A small brush with nylon bristles used for coating food with melted butter or other liquids

skewer—A thin wood or bamboo stick used to hold small pieces of meat or vegetables for broiling or grilling (see below)

steamer—A cooking utensil designed for cooking food with steam. Thai steamers have grates for holding food and tight-fitting lids.

tongs—A utensil used to grasp food

wok—A pot with a rounded bottom and sloping sides, ideally suited for stir-fried dishes. A large skillet is a fine substitute.

COOKING TERMS

beat—To stir rapidly in a circular motion

boil—To heat a liquid over high heat until bubbles form and rise rapidly to the surface

broil—To cook directly under a heat source so that the side of the food facing the heat cooks rapidly

fillet—A boneless piece of fish or meat

garnish—To decorate with a small piece of food

grill—To cook over hot charcoal

preheat—To allow an oven to warm up to a certain temperature before putting food into it

shred—To tear or cut into small pieces, either by hand or with a grater

simmer—To cook over low heat in liquid kept just below its boiling point

steam—To cook food with the steam from boiling water

stir-fry—To quickly cook bite-size pieces of food in a small amount of oil over high heat

SPECIAL INGREDIENTS

bay leaf—A seasoning made from the dried leaf of the bay (also called laurel) tree

bean sprouts—Sprouts from the mung bean. They can be bought either canned or fresh.

black mushrooms—Dried, fragrant mushrooms available at Oriental groceries

cardamom—A spice used in Indian-influenced curries

cayenne pepper—Ground hot red pepper

cellophane noodles—Thin noodles made from mung beans

cinnamon sticks—Cinnamon in stick form, used in Indian-influenced curries

clove—A ground spice used in Indian-influenced curries

coconut milk—The white, milky liquid extracted from coconut meat used to give a coconut flavor to foods. Canned coconut milk is available at Oriental groceries.

coriander—An herb used as a flavoring and as a decorative garnish. The dried powder is used in curries.

crushed red pepper flakes— Dried pieces of hot red peppers used to give a spicy flavor to foods

cumin— The seeds of an herb of the parsley family used in cooking to give food a pungent, slightly hot flavor

curry powder— A mixture of six or more spices that gives food a spicy taste. It is usually yellow.

extra-long-grain rice— A type of rice with very large grains. It absorbs more water than other types of rice and is dry and fluffy when cooked.

fish sauce— A bottled sauce made of processed fish, water, and salt. It is widely used in Thai cooking and is an ingredient in the popular sauce *nam pla prig*. Fish sauce is available at Oriental groceries and some supermarkets.

garam masala— An Indian-style curry powder. If unavailable, substitute ¼ teaspoon each of ground coriander, ground cumin, ground cloves, and pepper.

ginger root— A knobby, light brown root used to flavor foods

jalapeño pepper— A small, hot green chili pepper used to give food a spicy flavor

lemon grass— A tropical grass used as a flavoring in Thai foods. The lower, white part of the stalk is eaten. Both fresh and dried lemon grass are available at Oriental groceries. Dried lemon grass must be soaked in hot water 1 hour, drained, and chopped.

lumpia— Thin skins made of flour, water, and coconut oil used as wrappers for egg rolls

mint— Fresh or dried leaves of various mint plants used in cooking and for a garnish

rice noodles— Long, very thin noodles made from rice

scallion— A variety of green onion

sesame oil— The oil pressed from the sesame seed

soy sauce— A sauce made from soybeans and other ingredients that is used to flavor Oriental food

sweet basil leaves— Fresh or dried leaves of basil used in cooking and for a garnish

tofu— A processed curd made from soybeans

TYPICAL THAI MEALS

The Thai eat three meals a day—breakfast, lunch, and dinner—plus snacks of fruits, soups, noodle dishes, and sweets. Each meal follows a general pattern. Breakfast often includes boiled eggs, fried rice, and leftovers from yesterday's dinner. A noodle dish served with stir-fried vegetables is a typical lunch. Dinner usually consists of fresh salads, a dip or sauce, soup or curry, and side dishes of grilled, steamed, fried, or stir-fried vegetables with meat, fish, chicken, or seafood. The focal point of each meal is plenty of hot, fragrant rice.

Plan your Thai menus from the dishes in the groups below. Try to balance all the wonderful Thai flavors of hot, mild, salty, sweet, and sour. Remember that rice will cool the stinging bite of chilis! Each dish, no matter how simple, is always carefully cooked and arranged so it is as attractive as it is delicious.

ENGLISH	*THAI*	*PRONUNCIATION GUIDE*
Staples	***Aar Harnt Pra Jaam Wane***	ah hawn plah jem one
Nam Pla Prig	Nam Pla Prig	nahm plah prig
Rice	Kow	cow
Noodles	Guay Teow	goo-ay tee-ow
Noodle Dishes	***Guay Teow***	goo-ay tee-ow
Pineapple-Fish Noodles	Ka Nom Jeen Sour Nam	kah noom jeen sour nawm
Beef Noodles	Guay Teow Nua	goo-ay tee-ow new-ah
Salads	***Sa-lat***	sah-laht
Cucumber Salad	Sa-lat Tang Gua	sah-laht tang goo-ah
Spinach Salad	Sa-lat Pak Sa-pin-ach	sah-laht pawk sah-pin-ach

ENGLISH	THAI	PRONUNCIATION GUIDE
Soups and Curries	**Tom Chude, Gaeng**	tawm chood, gang
Lemon Chicken Soup	Tom Chude Gai Ma Noun	tawm chood guy moo now
Shrimp and Mushroom Soup	Tom Chude Goong Hdad	tawm chood goon head
Chicken Masman Curry	Gaeng Daeng Gai	gang dang guy
Panaeng Beef Curry	Panaeng Nua	pah-nang new-ah
Stir-fried and Fried Dishes	**Pad**	pod
Stir-fried Vegetables	Pad Pak	pod pawk
Stir-fried Meat with Sweet Basil	Nua Bye Ga Pon	new-ah by gah pow
Thai Egg Rolls	Poa Pee	pow pee-ah
Thai Fried Rice	Kow Pad Thai	cow pod tie
Grilled or Broiled Dishes	**Aar Han Pingg o Yaang**	ah hawn pin o yawng
Marinated Chicken	Gai Yaang	guy yawng
Satay	Satay	sah-tay
Steamed Dishes	**Aar Han Nong**	ah hawn nong
Thai Steamed Fish	Pla Nong	plah nong
Steamed Tofu	Tao Hu Nong	tah-oh hoo nong
Desserts	**Ka Nom**	kah noom
Thai Coconut Custard	Sang Ka Ya	sang kah yah
Stewed Bananas in Syrup	Glooy Boud Chee	gloo-ay boo-aht chee

STAPLES

Few cuisines offer the variety found in the cooking of Thailand. The flavors of Thai cooking range from mild to almost searingly hot, with plenty of dishes falling somewhere in between. These delicious and versatile staples are served with nearly every Thai dish and are a very important part of Thai cuisine.

Nam Pla Prig

Sauces are a specialty of Thailand, and there are many different versions. Nam pla prig, a sauce that combines the salty, sweet, and sour tastes that Thai people love, can be found on every table. It is used both as a dip and in place of salt, and the Thai sprinkle it on most dishes.

2 cloves garlic, crushed
1 teaspoon crushed red pepper flakes
4 tablespoons sugar
2 tablespoons fresh lime or lemon juice
    or 4 tablespoons white vinegar
4 tablespoons fish sauce

2 tablespoons water

1. Combine all ingredients in a small bowl. Stir to dissolve sugar. (If sauce is too salty or too strong, add more water, a tablespoon at a time, until it is the desired strength.)
2. Serve at room temperature in individual bowls. (*Nam pla prig* will keep for up to 2 weeks refrigerated in a tightly covered glass container.)

Makes about ½ cup

Rice/
Kow

Many varieties of rice are grown in Thailand. Short-grained sticky rice is often eaten by the central and northeastern Thai, and another especially delicious variety is jasmine, or fragrant, rice. But the backbone of every Thai meal is extra-long-grain rice.

2 cups extra-long-grain rice
2½ cups water

1. In a deep saucepan, bring rice and water to a boil over high heat. Boil, uncovered, for 2 to 3 minutes.
2. Cover pan and reduce heat to low. Simmer rice 20 to 25 minutes or until all water is absorbed.
3. Remove from heat. Keep covered and let rice steam 10 minutes.
4. Fluff rice with a fork and serve hot.

Serves 4

Noodles/
Guay Teow

Rice noodles are popular in Thailand and can be added to soups or to stir-fried, steamed, or simmered dishes, including curries. Very thin egg noodles are also eaten, as are cellophane noodles, which are made from mung beans. Although the Thai prefer fresh noodles, dried noodles can also be used.

3 cups water
1 7-ounce package rice noodles

1. In a large saucepan, bring water to a boil over high heat. Add rice noodles and return water to a boil.
2. Reduce heat to medium-high and cook noodles, uncovered, for 4 to 5 minutes or until soft.
3. Drain noodles in a colander and rinse in cold water. Serve immediately.

Serves 4

Noodles, a staple in the Thai diet, are served for lunch in such tasty dishes as pineapple-fish noodles *(back)* and beef noodles *(front)*.

NOODLE DISHES

Busy vendors sell delicious noodle dishes on the streets of Thailand. The noodles are not cut because long noodles are a sign of good luck. Noodles are usually served at lunch.

Pineapple-Fish Noodles/ Ka Nom Jeen Sour Nam

The pineapple has been popular in Thailand for hundreds of years. The Thai love its sweet-sour taste and use it as a vegetable in cooked dishes. For this recipe, sole, cod, haddock, or any other firm white fish can be used.

3 **tablespoons vegetable oil**
2 **pounds fish fillets, cut into bite-size pieces**
1 **clove garlic, finely chopped**
1 **teaspoon finely chopped fresh ginger**
1 **20-ounce can crushed pineapple, drained thoroughly**
1 **cup coconut milk**
2 **teaspoons fish sauce**
⅛ **teaspoon pepper**
1 **teaspoon sugar**
⅛ **teaspoon cayenne pepper**
   fresh mint and coriander for garnish (optional)

1. In a large skillet or wok, heat oil over high heat for 1 minute.
2. Add fish, garlic, and ginger. Cook, stirring constantly, for 3 minutes or until fish becomes white.
3. Add pineapple, coconut milk, fish sauce, pepper, sugar, and cayenne pepper and stir well. Cook, stirring constantly, for 2 minutes or until fish flakes easily.
4. Serve over hot rice noodles. Garnish with fresh mint and coriander.

Serves 4

Beef Noodles/
Guay Teow Nua

*This mildly flavored dish is traditionally
made with collard greens instead of broccoli,
a vegetable that has only recently found its
way to Thailand. Thinly sliced pork can
be substituted for the beef.*

3 **black mushrooms**
1½ **teaspoons cornstarch**
¼ **cup chicken broth or water**
3 **tablespoons vegetable oil**
1 **pound sirloin tip, thinly sliced**
½ **medium onion, peeled and thinly
    sliced**
1 **clove garlic, finely chopped**
2 **cups fresh broccoli, chopped, or 2
    cups frozen chopped broccoli,
    thawed**
1 **teaspoon soy sauce**
1 **teaspoon fish sauce**
⅛ **teaspoon pepper**

1. In a small bowl, soak black mushrooms
in hot water for 15 minutes. Drain well in
a colander and shred, discarding the stems.

2. In another small bowl, stir together
cornstarch and broth. Set aside.
3. In a large skillet or wok, heat 2 tablespoons oil over high heat for 1 minute.
Add meat and cook, stirring constantly,
for 2 to 3 minutes or until beef is tender
and nearly all brown. Place meat in a bowl
and set aside.
4. Wash skillet or wok and dry thoroughly.
5. Heat 1 tablespoon oil over high heat
for 1 minute. Add onion and garlic and
cook, stirring constantly, for 2 minutes or
until nearly tender.
6. Add broccoli and stir well. Stir corn-
starch-broth mixture and add to vegetables.
Cover, reduce heat to low, and simmer for
2 to 3 minutes or until broccoli is
crisp-tender.
7. Add mushrooms, soy sauce, fish sauce,
pepper, and meat. Cook, uncovered, over
medium heat, stirring frequently, for 1 to
2 minutes or until heated through.
8. Serve hot with rice noodles or
egg noodles.

Serves 4

SALADS

The Thai use many kinds of fresh, raw vegetables in their salads. Salads are always served at dinner, sometimes with a side sauce. Bits of cooked seafood, chicken, and pork can be added to enhance the flavor of the salad.

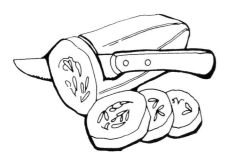

Cucumber Salad/ Sa-lat Tang Gua

This refreshing cucumber salad can be served with a meal or as a snack. It is a popular side dish with Thai egg rolls.

6 cherry tomatoes
2 cucumbers, peeled and shredded
2 green onions, shredded
2 tablespoons fish sauce
¼ teaspoon crushed red pepper flakes
2 tablespoons lime or lemon juice
2 tablespoons sugar
fresh coriander for garnish (optional)

1. Combine all ingredients except coriander in a large bowl. Lightly crush tomatoes, cucumbers, and green onions with a large spoon and mix well.
2. Garnish with fresh coriander and serve cold or at room temperature.

Serves 4

Spinach salad *(back)* **and cucumber salad** *(front)* **combine the mild, fresh flavor of raw vegetables with the hot taste of pepper.**

Spinach Salad/
Sa-lat Pak Sa-pin-ach

Collard greens are a common ingredient in Thai cooking and are usually used in this salad. In the United States, spinach is often easier to find and will make a tasty substitute. This party dish originated in the northeastern region of Thailand and is usually very spicy. Peanuts were introduced to Thai cooking by their neighboring country of Malaysia.

1 whole chicken breast
1½ tablespoons fish sauce
3 tablespoons sugar
3 tablespoons lime or lemon juice
⅛ teaspoon cayenne pepper
3 cups shredded fresh spinach
½ cup chopped roasted peanuts
½ cup peeled and shredded carrots

1. Rinse chicken breast under cool running water. Place in a large saucepan with enough water to cover and bring to a boil. Cover, reduce heat to low, and simmer for 30 minutes or until chicken is tender.

2. Remove chicken from pan with tongs. Place on a plate and cool for 15 minutes. When chicken is cool, remove meat from bones and shred into small pieces. Place chicken in a large bowl.

3. In a small bowl, mix fish sauce, sugar, lime juice, and cayenne pepper. Mix well until sugar dissolves.

4. Pour juice mixture over chicken and mix well.

5. Place spinach on a serving plate. Spoon chicken over spinach and top with carrots and peanuts. Serve at room temperature.

Serves 4

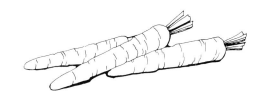

SOUPS AND CURRIES

For dinner, the Thai serve either a soup or a curry dish. Soups can be sour *(tom yam)* or "mixed." *Tom yam* includes lemon grass and lemon juice and sometimes lemon leaves. Mixed soups often have more ingredients than *tom yams* and include meat, poultry, or seafood, and vegetables.

Curries are the specialty of southern Thailand where chilis are included in every meal. There are four main types of curry. Red curry is named for the red chili peppers it contains; green curry is made with green chili peppers. Yellow curry and Muslim curry are very much alike, except that Muslim curry includes cinnamon, cloves, and cardamom. Curries are also classified as wet or dry. All wet curries include coconut milk for a sweeter and milder taste.

Lemon Chicken Soup/ Tom Chude Gai Ma Noun

The Thai love sharp flavors, and this popular soup, served throughout the country, satisfies with its delicious lemony tang. Shrimp, fish, or crab can be substituted for the chicken.

2 10¾-ounce cans (about 3 cups) chicken broth
1 stem lemon grass, cut into 1-inch pieces, or 1 tablespoon dried lemon grass, soaked
1 whole chicken breast, skinned, boned, and cut into bite-size pieces
1 cup cauliflower, cut into bite-size pieces, or 1 cup frozen chopped cauliflower, thawed
1 tomato, cut into 8 wedges
½ cup sliced fresh mushrooms or 1 3-ounce can sliced mushrooms, drained
1 teaspoon sugar
2 tablespoons fish sauce
1½ tablespoons lemon juice

1. In a large saucepan, bring broth to a boil over high heat. Add lemon grass and reduce heat to medium. Cook, uncovered, for 5 minutes or until broth has a lemon taste.

2. Add chicken, cauliflower, tomato, and mushrooms and cook, uncovered, for 3 to 4 minutes or until chicken and cauliflower are tender.

3. Add sugar, fish sauce, and lemon juice. Stir well.

4. Serve hot over rice or in individual soup bowls with rice on the side.

Serves 4

Shrimp and Mushroom Soup/ Tom Chude Goong Hdad

Shrimp is expensive in Thailand, so this lovely soup is reserved for special occasions. For a refreshing, sharp taste, add the juice of one lemon to the soup just before serving. You can also spice it up by adding crushed red pepper flakes.

2 10¾-ounce cans (about 3 cups) chicken broth
½ cup broccoli, cut into bite-size pieces, or ½ cup frozen chopped broccoli, thawed
½ cup coarsly chopped cabbage
1 pound fresh shrimp, peeled and deveined, or 1 pound frozen shrimp, thawed
1 cup sliced fresh mushrooms or 1 6-ounce can sliced mushrooms, drained
2 teaspoons fish sauce
¼ cup chopped scallions
⅛ teaspoon pepper

1. In a large saucepan, bring broth to a boil over high heat.

2. Add broccoli, cabbage, shrimp, and mushrooms and reduce heat to medium. Cook, uncovered, for 3 to 4 minutes or until shrimp become bright pink and curl tightly.

3. Add remaining ingredients. Cook for 30 seconds or until scallions are bright green.

4. Serve hot with rice.

Serves 4

A wide variety of spices, including cinnamon, cloves, garlic, and red pepper, gives Thai curries such as chicken masman curry *(back)* and panaeng beef curry *(front)* their distinctive taste.

Chicken Masman Curry/ Gaeng Daeng Gai

This dish was introduced into southern and central Thailand from India. The Thai have added their own touches and have transformed it into a distinctive and special Thai curry.

8 chicken thighs or legs, skinned, boned, and cut into bite-size pieces
½ teaspoon salt
1 teaspoon garam masala or ¼ teaspoon each: pepper, ground clove, ground cumin, ground coriander
¼ teaspoon cardamom
1 stalk lemon grass, finely chopped, or 1 tablespoon dried lemon grass, soaked
3 tablespoons vegetable oil
1 2-inch stick cinnamon or 1 teaspoon ground cinnamon
1 medium onion, peeled and cut into bite-size pieces
2 medium potatoes, peeled and cut into bite-size pieces
2 cups coconut milk
2 bay leaves
1 teaspoon sugar
2 tablespoons fish sauce
1 teaspoon lemon juice
¼ teaspoon crushed red pepper flakes
½ cup roasted peanuts for garnish

1. In a large bowl, mix chicken, salt, garam masala, cardamom, and lemon grass.
2. Heat oil in a large skillet over medium-high heat. Add cinnamon and onion and fry about 5 minutes or until onion turns brown. Add chicken mixture and fry, stirring constantly, until chicken is brown.
3. Add potatoes, coconut milk, and bay leaves and stir. Cover, reduce heat to low, and simmer for 20 minutes or until potatoes are tender.
4. Add sugar, fish sauce, lemon juice, and crushed red pepper flakes. Stir and cook for about 5 minutes to heat through.
5. Remove cinnamon and bay leaves from skillet. Garnish with peanuts and serve steaming hot with rice.

Serves 4 to 6

Panaeng Beef Curry/ Panaeng Nua

Panaeng, *a thick curry that does not include vegetables, originated in Malaysia. It can be made with either beef or chicken.*

2 cups coconut milk
1 pound stewing beef, cut into
       bite-size pieces
1 clove garlic, finely chopped
¼ teaspoon coriander powder
⅛ teaspoon pepper
¼ teaspoon salt
1 stalk lemon grass, finely chopped, or
       1 tablespoon dried lemon grass,
       soaked
3 tablespoons fish sauce
½ teaspoon lemon rind, finely chopped
2 tablespoons chunky peanut butter
1 tablespoon sugar
½ tablespoon crushed red pepper
       flakes
1 green onion, minced

1. In a large saucepan, bring coconut milk to a boil over high heat, stirring occasionally.

Reduce heat to low and simmer, uncovered, for 15 minutes, stirring occasionally.
2. Add remaining ingredients and stir. Cover and simmer over medium heat, stirring occasionally, for 1½ hours or until beef is tender.
3. Serve hot over rice.

Serves 4

STIR-FRIED AND FRIED DISHES

In Thailand, vegetables are often stir-fried to retain their flavor and nutrients. Although fresh vegetables are best for stir-frying, you can substitute the same amount of frozen vegetables, thawed. Sometimes meat, poultry, or seafood is also added. Stir-frying probably originated in China, and it was readily adapted by the Thai. It is a very quick cooking method that only takes minutes to complete, so have all of your ingredients chopped and ready before you start to stir-fry. In Thailand, both skillets and woks are used.

Stir-fried Vegetables/ Pad Pak

The Thai, have adopted the Chinese technique of stir-frying to preserve the color, fresh flavor, and texture of each vegetable. Only the best vegetables are selected. Any assortment of vegetables can be used in this recipe.

1 **tablespoon vegetable oil**
1 **small onion, peeled and sliced**
½ **cup broccoli, cut into bite-size pieces**
½ **cup cauliflower, cut into bite-size pieces**
½ **cup green beans, cut into bite-size pieces**
½ **cup sliced cabbage**
½ **cup sliced fresh mushrooms or 1 3-ounce can sliced mushrooms, drained**
1 **tablespoon fish sauce**
½ **tablespoon sugar**
¼ **teaspoon pepper**

1. In a large skillet or wok, heat oil over high heat for 1 minute.
2. Fry onion over high heat, stirring constantly, for 3 minutes or until tender.
3. Add broccoli, cauliflower, green beans, and cabbage. Cook for 2 to 3 minutes, stirring constantly. Add mushrooms and cook, stirring constantly, for 1 minute or until cabbage is crisp-tender.
4. Add fish sauce, sugar, and pepper and stir.
5. Serve hot with rice.

Serves 4

Stir-frying, one of the most popular cooking techniques in Thailand, preserves the fresh flavor of the ingredients in stir-fried meat with sweet basil *(left)* **and stir-fried vegetables** *(right)*.

Stir-fried Meat with Sweet Basil/ Nua Bye Ga Pon

The Thai usually use holy basil in this quick and easy dish, which originated thousands of years ago. Sweet basil is easier to find in the United States and is a good substitute. Chicken or shrimp can replace the beef.

12 sweet basil leaves, dried, or
        1 teaspoon dried basil
1 cup hot water
3 tablespoons vegetable oil
1 pound sirloin tip, thinly sliced
1 clove garlic, finely chopped
½ medium onion, peeled and sliced
½ cup sliced fresh mushrooms or
        1 3-ounce can sliced mushrooms,
        drained
2 jalapeño peppers, seeded and cut
        into quarters
1 tablespoon fish sauce
1 teaspoon sugar

1. In a small bowl, soak sweet basil in the hot water for 15 minutes. Drain and discard water.
2. In a large skillet or wok, heat 2 tablespoons oil over high heat for 1 minute. Add meat and cook over high heat, stirring constantly, until beef begins to turn brown. Place meat in a bowl and set aside.
3. Wash skillet or wok and dry thoroughly.
4. Heat 1 tablespoon oil over high heat for 1 minute. Add garlic, onion, mushrooms, and peppers and stir well. Cook, stirring frequently, for 1 minute or until mushrooms and peppers are soft.
5. Add beef, fish sauce, and sugar and stir well. Cook, stirring constantly, over medium heat for 2 minutes or until heated through.
6. Serve hot over rice.

Serves 4

Thai Egg Rolls/
Poa Pee

Delicious Thai egg rolls are always served at New Year's and for special occasions. The Thai use rice paper for a thin, crunchy wrapper. However, rice paper is sometimes difficult to find and is hard to work with. As a substitute, use lumpia papers, a thin flour-and-water wrapper. Look for lumpia in Oriental groceries or in the gourmet or frozen foods section of your supermarket.

3 black mushrooms
3½ ounces (one-half package) rice
**   noodles or cellophane noodles**
1 egg
½ pound ground pork
½ pound ground beef
1 cup peeled and shredded carrots
1 cup bean sprouts or
**   1 cup shredded cabbage**
½ medium onion, chopped
1 tablespoon fish sauce
¼ tablespoon pepper
½ clove garlic, finely chopped

1 teaspoon sugar
1 1-pound package lumpia, thawed
**   (about 25 wrappers)**
½ cup vegetable oil

1. In a small bowl, soak black mushrooms in hot water for 15 minutes. Drain well in a colander and shred, discarding the stems.
2. Soak noodles in hot water according to package directions. When soft, drain and cut into 2-inch lengths with a sharp knife or scissors.
3. In a large bowl, beat egg well. Add black mushrooms, noodles, pork, beef, carrots, bean sprouts, onion, fish sauce, pepper, garlic, and sugar. Mix well.
4. Place 1 wrapper on a flat surface. Cover remaining wrappers with a slightly damp kitchen towel so they don't dry out. Roll up according to directions on page 35.
5. In a large skillet or wok, heat oil over medium heat for 1 minute. Carefully place 3 rolls in oil and fry slowly for about 10 minutes or until golden brown. Turn and fry other side 10 minutes. Keep fried rolls warm in a 200° oven.

6. Cut each egg roll into 4 pieces. Serve hot with individual bowls of *nam pla prig* (page 18) or with sweet and sour sauce (page 38).

Makes 25 egg rolls

HOW TO WRAP EGG ROLLS

1. Have ready 1 beaten egg and a pastry brush.
2. Place about 1½ tablespoons of filling mixture just below center of skin.
3. Fold bottom edge over filling.
4. Fold in the two opposite edges so that they overlap.
5. Brush top edge corner with beaten egg. Roll up toward top edge and press edge to seal. Repeat with remaining wrappers.

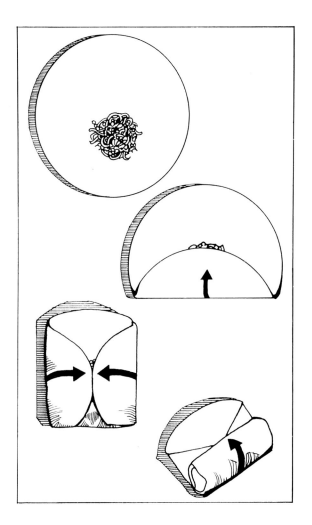

Thai fried rice makes a perfect accompaniment to crunchy Thai egg rolls served with *nam pla prig* or sweet and sour sauce.

Thai Fried Rice/ Kow Pad Thai

The original Thai brought this dish from China, and it quickly became a favorite family dish—with Thai touches, of course. It is good for using up leftovers because a variety of vegetables and meats or shrimp can be added or substituted. Although fried rice is often served as a breakfast or a lunch dish, it can become a party dish when you add 2 tablespoons of yellow curry powder. (The Thai consider yellow to be a party or celebration color.) To make the dish appear even more festive, garnish it with thin slices of cucumber and tomato.

2 eggs
4 tablespoons vegetable oil
½ medium onion, peeled and chopped
1 pound pork loin, thinly sliced
1 clove garlic, finely chopped
1 tomato, sliced into 8 wedges
2 green onions, thinly sliced
1 tablespoon fish sauce
1 teaspoon sugar
½ teaspoon pepper
½ teaspoon cayenne pepper (optional)
4 cups cold cooked rice

1. In a small bowl, beat eggs well.
2. In a large skillet or wok, heat 1 tablespoon oil over medium heat for 1 minute. Add beaten eggs and cook quickly, scrambling them with a spoon. Place eggs on a plate and set aside.
3. Clean skillet or wok. Heat 3 tablespoons oil over medium heat for 1 minute. Add onions, pork, and garlic and stir well. Cook, uncovered, for 2 minutes, stirring occasionally.
4. Add tomato and green onions and cook, stirring occasionally, for 2 minutes or until tomatoes soften.
5. Add fish sauce, sugar, pepper, and cayenne pepper and stir well.
6. Add rice, breaking apart any clumps. Mix well and cook, uncovered, for 6 to 8 minutes or until heated through.
7. Just before serving, add scrambled eggs and mix well. Serve hot.

Serves 4

GRILLED DISHES

Grilling is a cooking technique that the Thai may have learned from the people of Java. In Thailand, grilled dishes and snacks can be bought from street vendors, who quickly gather loyal followers for particularly tasty dips. You can cook these dishes on a charcoal grill or use your oven to broil or bake them.

Marinated Chicken/ Gai Yaang

In Thailand, pieces of meat, poultry, fish, and seafood are often grilled and served with a spicy dipping sauce. The leftover marinate is briefly boiled and served as a dip.

3 teaspoons sugar
2 tablespoons soy sauce
2 tablespoons fish sauce
1 teaspoon pepper
1 clove garlic, finely chopped
1 whole chicken, cut into 8 pieces

1. Mix all ingredients in a large bowl.

Cover and refrigerate 4 hours or overnight.
2. Preheat oven to broil.
3. Broil chicken for 40 to 45 minutes or until tender, turning often so that all sides are cooked evenly.
4. Serve chicken with *nam pla prig* (page 18) or with the following sweet and sour sauce.

Sweet and Sour Sauce:

1 cup sugar
¼ cup vinegar
1 teaspoon salt
½ cup water
1 tablespoon ketchup
¼ teaspoon crushed red pepper flakes

1. In a large saucepan, combine all ingredients. Stir constantly over high heat until sugar dissolves.
2. Serve at room temperature.

Serves 4

Satay

This tasty party dish is originally from Malaysia. The southern Thai add more curry, making the satay *spicier. In northern Thailand, it is served with sticky rice and stir-fried vegetables.*

1½ **pounds pork loin, thinly sliced**
    and cut into ½- by 2-inch strips
2 **teaspoons sugar**
1 **tablespoon fish sauce**
1½ **teaspoons yellow curry powder**
¼ **teaspoon pepper**
1½ **cups coconut milk**
4 **tablespoons chunky peanut butter**
2 **teaspoons fish sauce**

1. In a large mixing bowl, combine the first 5 ingredients. Mix well, cover, and refrigerate for 4 hours or overnight.
2. In a deep saucepan, mix remaining ingredients. Bring to a boil over high heat, stirring constantly until well mixed. Place in a bowl, cover, and refrigerate.
3. Soak 12 small wooden skewers in water for ½ hour or until ready to use.
4. Preheat oven to broil.
5. Thread pork onto skewers accordian style. When oven is preheated, broil pork for 8 to 10 minutes or until done, turning often so all sides are cooked evenly.
6. Serve hot with bowls of the coconut-peanut butter sauce for dipping. *Satay* is delicious with a cucumber salad or with the following cucumber sauce.

Cucumber Sauce:

½ **cup vinegar**
1 **cup sugar**
1 **teaspoon salt**
1 **cup peeled and thinly sliced**
    cucumber

1. In a medium saucepan, combine vinegar, sugar, and salt and bring to a boil over high heat. Stir until sugar dissolves. Remove from heat and let cool, uncovered, to room temperature.
2. Pour sauce over cucumber immediately before serving.

Serves 4

STEAMED DISHES

Steaming is a popular cooking method for seafood, especially fish, and retains much of the nutrients and natural flavor of the ingredients. If you don't have an Oriental metal steamer, set a heat resistant bowl containing the food to be steamed into a flat pan. Pour about ½ cup of boiling water into the pan. Cover the bowl and place the pan and the dish in a pre-heated 350° oven for the amount of time given in the recipe.

Thai Steamed Fish/ Pla Nong

This dish probably originated in China and is now popular throughout Thailand. It is mild enough to be enjoyed by all members of the family. Any white fish, including sole, cod, or haddock can be used.

3 black mushrooms
1 teaspoon finely chopped fresh ginger
2 teaspoons soy sauce
½ teaspoon pepper
¼ cup chopped scallions
1 whole fish, cleaned, or 2 pounds white-fish fillets, cut into bite-size pieces

1. In a small bowl, soak black mushrooms in hot water for 15 minutes. Drain well in a colander and shred, discarding the tough stems. Set aside.
2. In a heat-resistant bowl, combine mushrooms, ginger, soy sauce, pepper, scallions, and fish and mix well.
3. Place ½ cup water in a steamer and bring to a boil over high heat. Place bowl with fish mixture into steamer. Cover and steam over medium heat for 40 to 45 minutes.
4. Serve hot with rice. Spoon juices over fish and rice.

Serves 4

Steamed Tofu/
Tao Hu Nong

This family dish is not served to guests. It originated in central Thailand and is especially popular with Chinese Thai.

1 1-pound package firm-style tofu, cut into 1-inch cubes
½ pound ground pork or shrimp
2 tablespoons fish sauce
¼ teaspoon salt
¼ teaspoon pepper
¼ teaspoon crushed red pepper flakes (optional)
½ teaspoon sugar
1 teaspoon sesame oil

1. In a heat resistant bowl, combine all ingredients and mix well.
2. Place ½ cup water in a steamer and bring to a boil over high heat. Place bowl containing tofu mixture into steamer. Cover and let steam over medium heat for 25 minutes. Serve hot with rice.

Serves 4

Thai steamed fish and steamed tofu are nutritious dishes that are easy to make.

The delicious flavor of coconuts and bananas, two fruits native to Thailand, make Thai coconut custard and stewed bananas in syrup popular choices for a snack or dessert.

DESSERTS

Coconut milk and palm sugar, as well as sweet or sticky rice, mung beans, and bananas, are often used in Thai desserts. Desserts are of two types, liquid or dry. Most liquid desserts are made with fruits and a sweet liquid. Dry desserts have no syrup and are often custards or small cake-like treats.

Thai Coconut Custard/ Sang Ka Ya

This dry dessert is a light, yet rich, treat at the end of dinner. It is also a popular snack. Buttercup squash is excellent in this custard, but other kinds of squash or pumpkin can also be used.

4 eggs
¼ cup brown sugar
¼ cup white sugar
1 cup coconut milk
1 cup thinly sliced winter squash, seeds and rind removed

1. In a deep bowl, beat eggs well.
2. Add brown and white sugars and stir until dissolved.
3. Add coconut milk and squash and stir well.
4. Pour mixture into a 9- by 9-inch baking pan or a 9- or 10-inch pie plate.
5. Place ½ cup water into a steamer and bring to a boil over high heat. Place pie plate containing custard into steamer. Cover and steam over high heat for 30 minutes.
6. Serve at room temperature.

Serves 4

Stewed Bananas in Syrup/ Glooy Boud Chee

The hottest months in Thailand, April and May, are when this liquid dessert is the most popular. This dessert is served as a sweet treat at the end of a meal or as a snack.

1½ **cups coconut milk**
⅛ **teaspoon salt**
¼ **cup sugar**
½ **cup water**
4 **firm medium bananas, peeled and halved crosswise**

1. In a small bowl, mix coconut milk and salt. Set aside.
2. In a large saucepan, bring sugar and water to a boil over high heat, stirring constantly. Add bananas and reduce heat to medium. Cook, uncovered, for 8 to 10 minutes or until liquid is clear and bananas are tender.
3. Pour the coconut milk over the bananas.
4. Serve at room temperature.

Serves 4

THE CAREFUL COOK

Whenever you cook, there are certain safety rules you must always keep in mind.

1. Always wash your hands before handling food.
2. Thoroughly wash all raw vegetables and fruits to remove dirt and chemicals.
3. Use a cutting board when cutting up vegetables and fruits. Don't cut them up in your hand! And be sure to cut in a direction *away* from you and your fingers.
4. Long hair or loose clothing can catch fire if brought near the burners of a stove. If you have long hair, tie it back before cooking.
5. Turn all pot handles toward the back of the stove so that you will not catch your sleeves or jewelry on them. This is especially important when younger brothers and sisters are around. They could easily knock off a pot and get burned.
6. Always use a pot holder to steady hot pots or to take pans out of the oven. Don't use a wet cloth on a hot pan because the steam it produces could burn you.
7. Lift the lid of a steaming pot with the opening away from you so that you will not get burned.
8. If you get burned, hold the burn under cold running water. Do not put grease or butter on it. Cold water helps to take the heat out, but grease or butter will only keep it in.
9. If grease or cooking oil catches fire, throw baking soda or salt at the bottom of the flame to put it out. (Water will *not* put out a grease fire.) Call for help, and try to turn all the stove burners to "off."

HANDLING CHILIES

Fresh chilies have to be handled with care because they contain oils that can burn your eyes or mouth. After working with chilies, be sure not to touch your face until you have washed your hands thoroughly with soap and water. To be extra cautious, wear rubber gloves while fixing chilies. The way you cut the peppers will affect their "hotness." If you take out the seeds, the flavor will be sharp but not fiery. If you leave the seeds in, beware!

METRIC CONVERSION CHART

WHEN YOU KNOW	MULTIPLY BY	TO FIND
MASS (weight)		
ounces (oz)	28.0	grams (g)
pounds (lb)	0.45	kilograms (kg)
VOLUME		
teaspoons (tsp)	5.0	milliliters (ml)
tablespoons (Tbsp)	15.0	milliliters
fluid ounces (oz)	30.0	milliliters
cup (c)	0.24	liters (l)
pint (pt)	0.47	liters
quart (qt)	0.95	liters
gallon (gal)	3.8	liters
TEMPERATURE		
Fahrenheit (°F) temperature	5/9 (after subtracting 32)	Celsius (°C) temperature

COMMON MEASURES AND THEIR EQUIVALENTS

3 teaspoons = 1 tablespoon

8 tablespoons = ½ cup

2 cups = 1 pint

2 pints = 1 quart

4 quarts = 1 gallon

16 ounces = 1 pound

INDEX

(recipes indicated by **bold face** *type)*

ABOUT THE AUTHORS

A native Thai, **Supenn Harrison** came to Minneapolis, Minnesota, in 1972. She started her first Thai restaurant in 1979 and opened a second in 1983. Harrison enjoys swimming, camping, and teaching Thai cooking classes.

Judy Monroe, born in Duluth, Minnesota, has mastered several Southeast Asian cuisines, including Thai cooking. A graduate of the University of Minnesota, Monroe is currently a biomedical librarian and a freelance writer. In her spare time, she enjoys ethnic cooking, baking, gardening, and reading.

Cooking the **CHINESE** Way
Cooking the **ENGLISH** Way
Cooking the **FRENCH** Way
Cooking the **GERMAN** Way
Cooking the **GREEK** Way
Cooking the **HUNGARIAN** Way
Cooking the **INDIAN** Way
Cooking the **ISRAELI** Way
Cooking the **ITALIAN** Way
Cooking the **JAPANESE** Way
Cooking the **LEBANESE** Way
Cooking the **MEXICAN** Way
Cooking the **NORWEGIAN** Way
Cooking the **POLISH** Way
Cooking the **RUSSIAN** Way
Cooking the **SPANISH** Way
Cooking the **THAI** Way
Cooking the **VIETNAMESE** Way